The Joy of Clarinet

THE JOY OF CLARINET is a colorful, well-balanced repertoire of appealing solo pieces, with piano accompaniment, designed for the beginning and intermediate grade player. Here are familiar themes by the masters, classic and modern, folk tunes, favorite standard songs and popular melodies of today. The variety is both pleasing and educational.

In general, the selections follow a graded sequence. The first few pieces can be played as early as the second or third month of study. The shorter selections may be combined into groups of two or three, and are playable in sequence to form a longer, more impressive recital unit. A few suggestions as to such groupings may be found on the bottom of this page.

This collection was expertly edited by Jerome Goldstein, former member of the Pittsburgh and Dallas Symphonies, presently a well known band director and educator. The piano accompaniments, always simple and well-sounding, are by Denes Agay, whose work in the field of piano teaching materials is widely known and respected.

THE JOY OF CLARINET is an excellent supplement and companion book to any good clarinet method. It provides carefully selected, enjoyable pieces for the technical and musical development of the young player.

Here are a few examples for effective grouping of the shorter selections:

Down In The Valley   The Trout
Red River Valley   Chit-Chat

Lament   Melody
Maypole Dance   Comedians' Galop

The Lonesome Road   Theme from "Pathetique Symphony"
When The Saints Come Marchin' In   Capriccio Italien

Vilia   Aria from "Don Giovanni"
Rumanian Rhapsody   Rondino

Sarabande   Aura Lee
Bourrée   Roses From The South

Blow The Man Down   Finale from Symphony No. 1
House of The Rising Sun   German Dance
Folk Boogie   The Bagpipers

Distributed throughout the world by:
Music Sales Corporation
257 Park Avenue South, New York, NY 10010, USA.

Music Sales Limited
8/9 Frith Street, London W1V 5TZ, England.

Music Sales Pty Limited
120 Rothschild Avenue, Rosebery, NSW2018, Australia.

CONTENTS

1. The Carman's Whistle

William Byrd
(1543 - 1623)

2. Down In The Valley

Folk Song

3. Red River Valley

Cowboy Song

4. Blow The Man Down

Sea Chantey

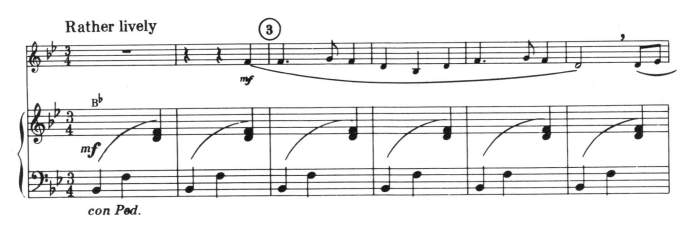

5. Folk Boogie

6. House Of The Rising Sun

Folk Ballad

7. The Riddle Song

Folk Song

8. Roses From The South

Theme

Johann Strauss

9. Lament

Béla Bartók

10. Maypole Dance

Béla Bartók

11. Give My Regards To Broadway

George M. Cohan

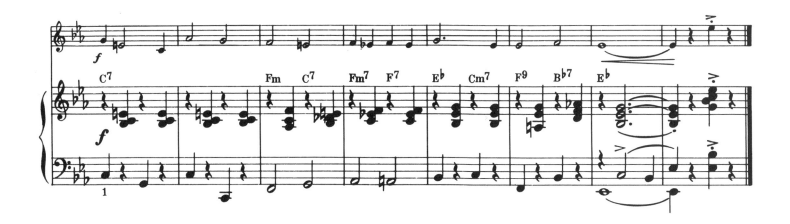

12. The Lonesome Road

Words by Gene Austin
Music by Nathaniel Shilkret

13. We Three Kings Of Orient Are

John Henry Hopkins, Jr.

14. Plaisir d'Amour

Jean Paul Martini
(1741 - 1816)

Andantino

D.S. al Fine

15. When The Saints Come Marchin' In

Spiritual

16. Aura Lee

George R. Pulton

Simply, tenderly

17. Chit-Chat

Dmitri Kabalevsky

18. Marian

Calypso Song

19. The Bagpipers

Theme from Symphony No. 104

Joseph Haydn

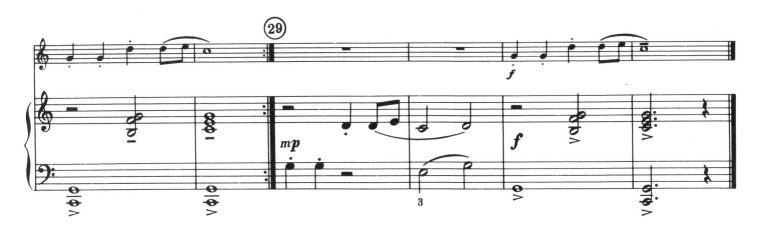

20. German Dance

Ludwig van Beethoven

21. The Trout

Franz Schubert

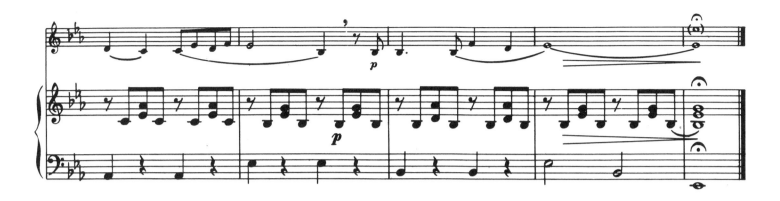

22. Melody

Robert Schumann

23. Vilia

From "The Merry Widow"

Franz Lehár

Moderately

24. Rumanian Rhapsody

Georges Enesco

25. The Comedians' Galop

Dmitri Kabalevsky

D.C. al Fine

26. Black Is The Color

Of My True Love's Hair

Folk Song

Slowly

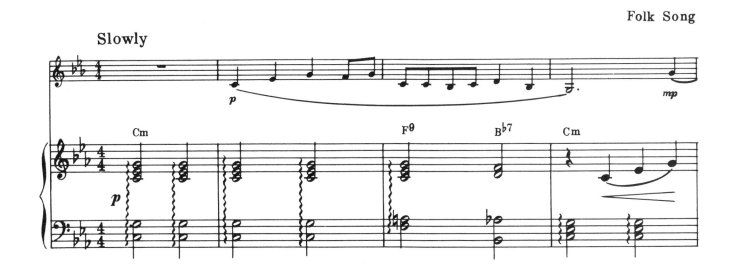

27. Sarabande

Arcangelo Corelli
(1653 - 1713)

Lento espressivo

28. Bourrée

Johann Krieger
(1652 - 1735)

29. Aria From "Don Giovanni"

Là Ci Darem La Mano

Wolfgang A. Mozart

30. Theme From "Pathetique" Symphony

Peter I. Tchaikovsky

31. Venetian Boat-Song

Felix Mendelssohn – Bartholdy

32. Finale From Symphony No.1

Theme

Johannes Brahms

33. Capriccio Italien

Theme (Solo or Duet)

Peter I. Tchaikovsky

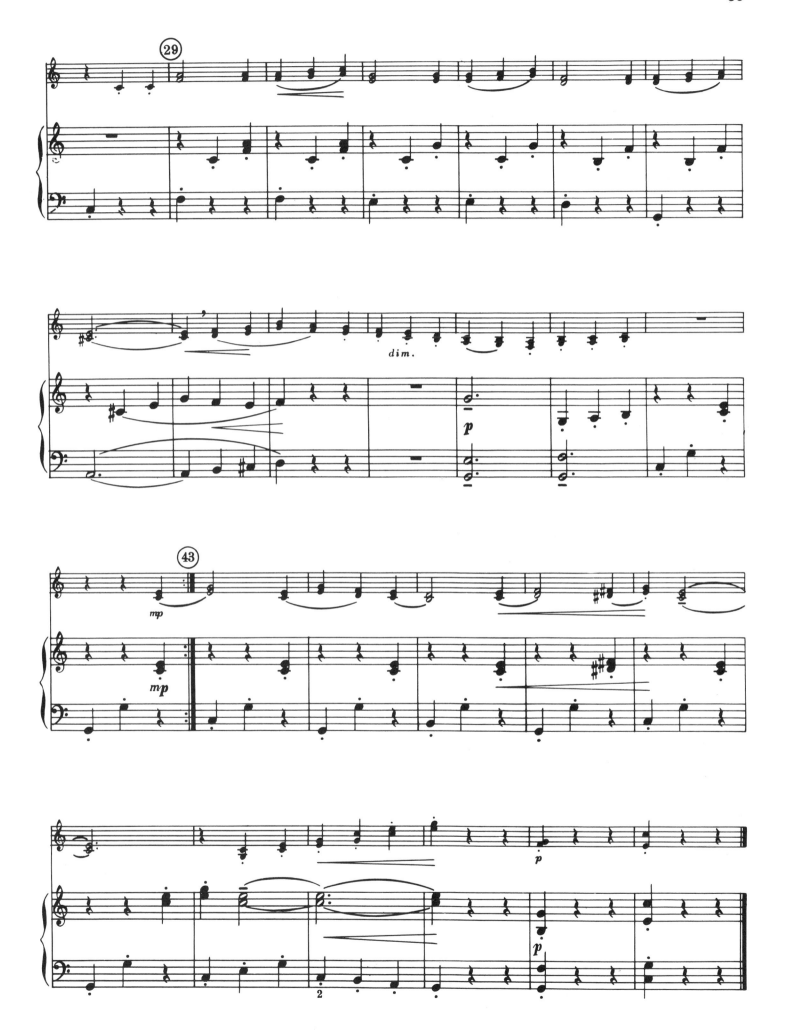

34. Gypsy Life

Csardas

V. Monti

35. Romance
From "The Pearl Fishers"
(Solo or Duet)

Georges Bizet

36. Variations On "Little Brown Jug"

Gerald Martin

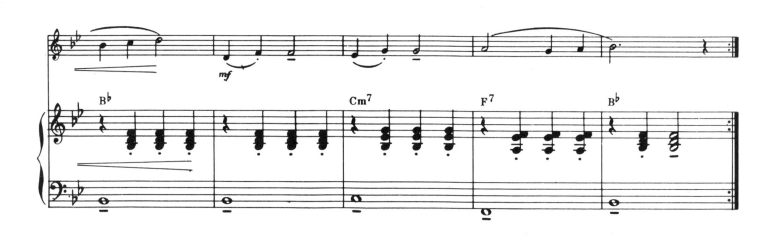

37. Musette

Johann Sebastian Bach

38. Nocturne

Frédéric Chopin

39. A Touch Of Blues

Gerald Martin

40. Rondino
Theme from Divertimento No.14

Wolfgang A. Mozart

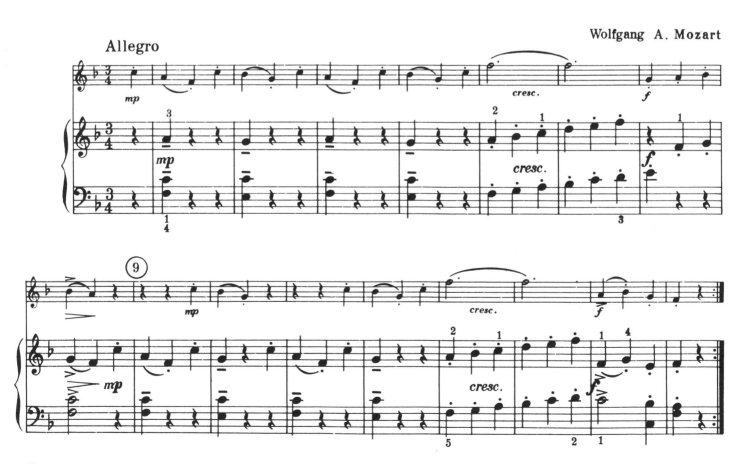

48

Printed and bound in Great Britain by
Caligraving Limited Thetford Norfolk
9/99 (35201)